UNIVERSITY
GLOUCESTER

the
rockpool

the beach

high tide mark

Bellamy's Changing World: The Rockpool
was conceived, edited and designed by Frances Lincoln Limited
Apollo Works, 5 Charlton Kings Road, London NW5 2SB

Text © 1988 by Botanical Enterprises Publications Ltd.
Illustrations © Jill Dow 1988

First published in Great Britain by
Macdonald and Co. (Publishers) Ltd,
Greater London House,
Hampstead Road,
London NW1 7RX
A BPCC plc Company

British Library Cataloguing in Publication Data

Bellamy, David *1933* —
The rockpool — (Bellamy's Changing World: 4)
1. Tide pool ecology — Juvenile literature
I. Title   II. Dow, Jill   III. Series
574.9   QH541.5.S35

574.9

ISBN 0-356-13569-1

Printed and bound in Italy

Design and Art Direction Debbie Mackinnon

Frances Lincoln Ltd. would like to thank
Pippa Rubinstein, Trish Burgess, Sarah Mitchell,
Kathy Henderson, Kathryn Cave, Stephen Pollock
and Jackie Westbrook for help with the series.

Bellamy's Changing World
The
Rockpool

David Bellamy

with illustrations by Jill Dow

Macdonald

It's a fine day by the sea and there's a lot to do. When you get tired of building sandcastles and playing, you can always go exploring.

The girl has seen a stranded jellyfish drying out among the seaweed and shells near today's high tide mark. She is going to fetch her bucket to carry the jellyfish to the rockpool. She's very careful not to touch it with her bare hands because it might sting her.

At high tide, most of the beach is covered, and the sea washes in and out of the rockpool twice a day. There are hundreds of living things in the pool waiting to be discovered. All you have to do is look.

The water in the pool is so clear you can see right down to the bottom. Look carefully – there is a large starfish and a small fish called a blenny hiding among the seaweed. Even the shells can hold surprises. That whelk shell has been taken over by a hermit crab – it uses the shell as a home to protect the rear part of its body, which has no hard covering. When the crab is disturbed it retreats inside the shell and closes up the entrance with its large claw.

The jellyfish is now floating about among the seaweed in the pool. Its tentacles are covered with thousands of stinging cells. These are used to paralyse small creatures before it eats them. The blenny had better stay out of the way! Crabs and starfish don't have to worry because their tough outer covering protects them from stings.

The red anemones are relatives of the jellyfish and unfurl their frill of stinging tentacles in the water in search of very tiny fish and shellfish to eat.

The rocks are covered with seaweeds of all shapes and sizes. They cling to the rocks with stick-tight pads called holdfasts, and their slippery fronds slide about in the waves without getting torn. The brown kelps and wracks are tough and can live out of water for short periods. The red seaweeds are more delicate and live only in the deepest parts of the pool.

While the tide is out, the whelks and winkles stay either in the pool or in the dampness under the wracks on the rocks. Seaweeds make oxygen during the day, which the animals in the pool need in order to live. The green seaweeds are very good at this – look at all the silver bubbles of oxygen.

The limpets on top of the rocks have clamped themselves down so that they don't dry up when the tide is out, but the ones in the water are moving around slowly. Can you see their feelers? They graze on the small seaweeds near their home base and leave a trail of tiny marks. All the limpets will clamp down tightly in stormy weather, or if threatened by a gull.

Limpets, whelks and winkles are members of the snail family. So are mussels and oysters, although they have two shells instead of only one. They feed by opening their hinged shells and drawing water through, filtering out tiny particles of food. This also helps keep the water in the pool clean. The mussels can't move away because they are anchored to the rock by strong threads.

1 limpet   2 whelk
3 winkle   4 mussel

As we grow bigger we have to buy new shoes and clothes. As crabs grow, they have to get rid of their old wraparound shells and grow new ones, one size up. The crab hiding in a crevice is waiting for its new shell to get hard. Only then will it come out to feed. Can you see its old shell on the bottom of the pool?

Shrimps and prawns have lighter shells than crabs and they can dart about quickly to catch their food.

The barnacles you can see on the rocks, and even on top of some of the limpets, may look like snails but are really related to shrimps and crabs. Look closely and you'll see their tiny feathery legs sticking out of the opening at the top; these scoop in food particles from the water. If you could put your ear very close to the pool you'd be able to hear the rustle of those tiny legs.

The starfish are at work feeding. One is using its long tube feet to ease open the shells of mussels so that it can eat the soft parts inside. The spiky creatures on the rocks are sea urchins, relatives of the starfish. They have tube feet, too, and they move around the pool scraping up anything that is good to eat. If you go paddling, watch out for sea urchins – they can't eat you, but those spines are sharp.

This hermit crab has outgrown its old shell and is in the middle of moving house. It had better be quick – a big crab is waiting to pounce.

Many small fish are trapped in the pool when the tide goes out. Some are hiding among the weeds, but flat fish like baby plaice and flounders lie on the bottom, partly buried in the sand. They can change the colour and the pattern of their spots to help make them invisible and so protect them from other fish that might want to eat them.

The female stickleback has laid her eggs in a nest made of
seaweed, and the male is looking after them by wafting
clean water, full of oxygen, through the nest with his fins.

1 butterfish   2 plaice   3 stickleback   4 blenny

It's late afternoon and a storm is brewing. The yachts are hurrying back to the shelter of the bay and the people on the beach have all gone home.

The tide is coming in now and big waves are crashing on the rocks by the pool. The mussels will need their strong anchor threads and the limpets will have to clamp down and hold on very tightly until the storm is past.

There'll be no fun and games on the beach today. During last night's storm, oil leaked from a struggling tanker and washed up on the beach. Now everything is covered with the thick black oil.

Oil is bad enough on your clothes and skin, but for the animals of the seashore it is a nightmare. It gums up the gills of sticklebacks, shrimps and crabs so they can't breathe. It sticks the seabirds' feathers together so that they can't fly and, if the birds preen themselves, they will swallow oil and die. The lucky ones are washed up on the shore and taken away to be cleaned, but, for many, help has come too late.

The rockpool is a disaster area. The mussels and most of the barnacles have suffocated. The delicate tube feet of the starfish and sea urchins are poisoned by the oil and they die. So do the beautiful anemones.

Only a few creatures escape. Let's hope the fish swam out to sea before it was too late. The hermit crab is out of danger and some of the limpets have survived, tightly clamped down until the worst of the pollution had passed. They are now grazing on the seaweed in safe places between the oil slicks.

Each high tide will wash away some of the oil but the surviving creatures of the rockpool will have to live a life tainted with oil for a long time to come.

A year later, the rockpool is getting back to normal. There are more green seaweeds than before, because they grow very quickly and there are fewer limpets to eat them. Thousands of tiny barnacles cover the rocks and there are new colonies of mussels in the crevices. Blennies are back again, too.

You may still get patches of oil on your clothes when you play on the beach or explore the rocks, but the pool has come back to life. With luck, the creatures that live there will never have to face such disaster again.